D0984919

CONCORD AND LEXINGTON

CONCORD AND LEXINGTON

 **DILLON PRESS**
New York

Maxwell Macmillan Canada
Toronto

Maxwell Macmillan International
New York   Oxford   Singapore   Sydney

by Judy Nordstrom

Acknowledgments

The author wishes to acknowledge the enthusiastic scholarship of a great lover of history, Mrs. Marcia Moss, curator at the Concord Free Public Library, without whose assistance this book would not have been possible.

Photo Credits

Cover photos courtesy of the National Park Service—Dennis Dostie. James Blank: title page, 52, 57, 61, 64; Ann C. Somers and N. Loring Webster: 8, 35, 40, 47, 49, 60, 62; Gerald A. Nordstrom: 13, 27, 29, 37, 65; National Portrait Gallery, Smithsonian Institution: 19, 21; Concord Free Public Library: 43.

Library of Congress Cataloging-inPublication Data

Nordstrom, Judy.
    Concord and Lexington / by Judy Nordstrom. — 1st ed.
      p.   cm. — (Places in American history)
    Includes index.
    Summary: Describes the first battles of the Revolutionary War, the events leading up to the conflict, and the monuments that have been erected to commemorate this pivotal point in history.
    ISBN 0-87518-567-3
    1. Concord, Battle of, 1775—Juvenile literature. 2. Lexington, Battle of, 1775—Juvenile literature. [1. Concord, Battle of, 1775. 2. Lexington, Battle of, 1775. 3. United States—History—Revolution, 1775-1783—Campaigns.] I. Title. II. Series.
E241.C7N66   1993
973.3'311—dc20   92-23392

Dillon Press
Macmillan Publishing Company
866 Third Avenue
New York, NY 10022

Maxwell Macmillan Canada, Inc.
1200 Eglinton Avenue East
Suite 200
Don Mills, Ontario M3C 3N1

Macmillan Publishing Company is part of the Maxwell Communication Group of Companies.

First edition

Printed in the United States of America

10 9 8 7 6 5 4 3 2 1

★ ★ ★ ★ ★ ★ ★ ★ ★ ★ ★ ★ ★ ★ ★ ★ ★ ★ ★

CONTENTS

Concord and Lexington

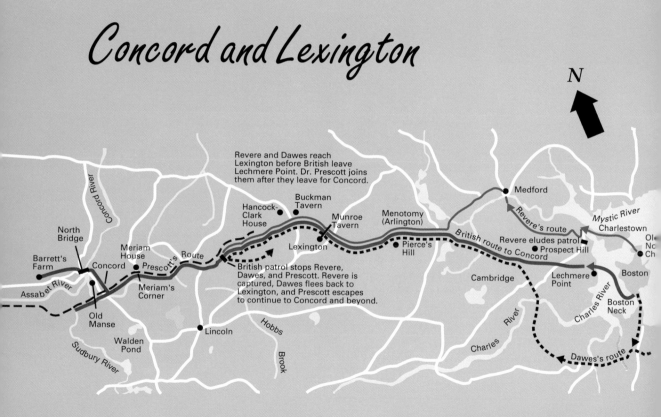

N

Revere and Dawes reach Lexington before British leave Lechmere Point. Dr. Prescott joins them after they leave for Concord.

Concord River

North Bridge

Barrett's Farm

Meriam House

Concord

Meriam's Corner

Prescott's Route

Assabet River

Old Manse

Walden Pond

Sudbury River

Lincoln

Hobbs Brook

Hancock-Clark House

Buckman Tavern

Munroe Tavern

Lexington

British patrol stops Revere, Dawes, and Prescott. Revere is captured, Dawes flees back to Lexington, and Prescott escapes to continue to Concord and beyond.

Menotomy (Arlington)

Pierce's Hill

British route to Concord

Cambridge

Charles River

Charles River

Charles

Charles River

Medford

Revere's route

Revere eludes patrol

Prospect Hill

Lechmere Point

Dawes's route

Mystic River

Charlestown

Ol Nc Ch

Boston

Boston Neck

Massachusetts

Concord-Lexington area

Routes of the British Forces and the Colonial Messengers

▪ ▪ ▪ ▪ Dawes's route
▬▬▬ British route
– – – Prescott's route
▬▬▬ Revere's route

CHAPTER 1

ON THE EVE OF A REVOLUTION

The winter of 1775 had been mild in the Massachusetts Bay Colony. By mid-April the weather was warmer than usual and the trees were already budding. Across the rolling hills of Concord, children played in the meadows. Nearby their fathers worked hard to prepare the fields for spring planting.

As the farmers worked the land, others in Concord turned to more urgent tasks. Fifteen-year-old Meliscent Barrett, granddaughter of the militia's Colonel James Barrett, showed the town's young women how to make rifle cartridges. Tradesmen neglected their businesses to concentrate on making rifles and muskets. A brewer hid extra kegs of flour in his malthouse.

Wright Tavern, one of the several places in Concord where rebel leaders could meet

Housewives cured whole sides of beef and pork, and coopers fashioned barrels to store them in. In short, Concord was preparing for war.

Since February 1 the town's nine inns and boardinghouses had been filled with members of the Second Provincial Congress. The congress was a body of men from all the towns and cities of Massachusetts. They had joined together to protest the government of King George III of England. The group had no power to pass laws, but most people in the colony followed its advice and recommendations. Now the Provincial Congress was meeting to try to agree on the rules and regulations for forming an army.

The American colonies had never had an army. Since their founding, they had relied on local militias, made up of all able-bodied men, for defense. Many of the representatives at the Second Provincial Congress argued against forming an army—they wanted no part of fighting against the king's troops. By April 1, after long debate, the meetings had stalled.

Then, on April 3, a letter arrived in Concord for rebel leader Samuel Adams. An American agent in England warned that the British Parliament had voted to support King George in all efforts to control the colonies. General Thomas Gage, the new military governor of Massachusetts, was to receive even more soldiers to add to the 4,000 British troops already in Boston. Gage was instructed to maintain order, no matter what.

On April 10 the Provincial Congress sent a message to every town in Massachusetts: Local militias should be ready to respond in case of emergency. The next day riders left Concord for Rhode Island, New Hampshire, and Connecticut. They carried urgent messages asking those colonies to join Massachusetts in the creation of a colonial army. On April 15 the Second Provincial Congress ended its meetings.

Under the light of a full moon, Sam Adams and his friend and fellow rebel John Hancock rode from Concord to Lexington. There they stayed as guests of the town's minister, the Reverend Jonas Clark. Adams and Hancock planned to start for Philadelphia within a week for the second meeting of the Continental Congress. At this larger congress, with delegates from all the colonies, they hoped to persuade others to join their fight for independence.

The events of the next four days would do more to rally others to their cause than Adams and Hancock ever could have imagined.

On April 16 Dr. Joseph Warren, a Boston physician and political organizer, received news from rebel spies. All British soldiers stationed in Boston who were on leave had been ordered back to active duty. Longboats in the mouth of the Charles River had been repaired and tied up to the warships. It looked as if the British were up to something.

Fearing that the British planned a march to Lexington to capture Adams and Hancock, Warren sent for his friend Paul Revere. The Boston silversmith often carried messages for the rebel cause. Now he rode to Lexington to warn the two rebel leaders.

On his way home, Revere stopped in Charlestown, across the Charles River from

Boston. There he met with Colonel William Conant of the Charlestown militia. Revere promised to alert the militia if he received news that the British were marching from Boston. One lantern would be hung in the steeple of Boston's Old North Church if the march was "by land," two if the troops left in boats, or "by sea."

Two days after Revere's return, rebel spies learned the true destination of the British army. General Gage was preparing for a dawn raid on Concord—one of the places where the colonists stored their ammunition. Crossing the Charles River and marching west toward their goal, Gage's men would have to pass through Lexington.

Summoned again by Dr. Warren, Paul Revere began his famous "midnight ride." Shouting his warning at each house along the way, he galloped the 11 miles (18 kilometers) from Boston to Lexington. An hour later members of the militia stood in ranks on Lexington Green, even

The Old North Church in Boston. The lanterns that signaled to Paul Revere were hung in the upper window of the steeple.

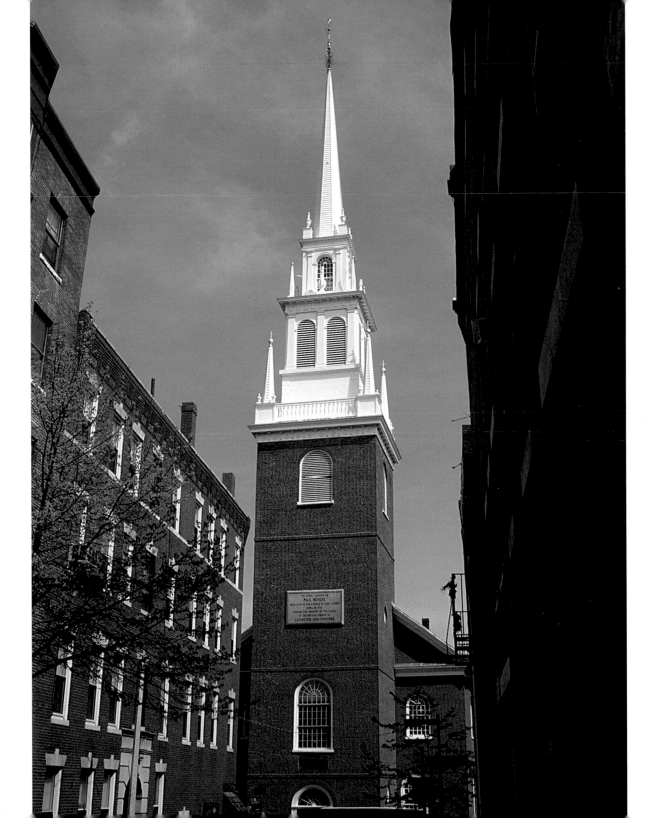

as church bells rang the first alarm 6 miles (10 kilometers) beyond in Concord.

In the predawn darkness of April 19, 1775, militiamen stood their ground in Lexington and Concord. By day's end many of these brave men would be the first to fall in the Revolutionary War—the war that began with the "shot heard 'round the world."

CHAPTER 2

IT DIDN'T HAPPEN OVERNIGHT

The decision to fight the British was not an easy one, but it was one that had been coming for several years. The American colonies' disputes with England had begun shortly after King George III took the throne in 1760. The 22-year-old king found himself the ruler of a nation at war. England was battling the French and the American Indians in Canada over ownership of North America. By the time the last battle of the war ended in 1763, England had defeated its enemies, but it was deeply in debt.

King George was determined to rebuild the royal treasury. Taxes in England were already high. The Americans, on the other hand, had not paid taxes directly to the British government in more than 100 years. The colonies instead were "indirectly" taxed, through customs duties, or fees paid on goods they imported.

That situation changed in 1764, when the British Parliament began to pass a series of resolutions, or laws, to raise more money in the American colonies. One of these resolutions was the Stamp Act, which went into effect in 1765. Colonists were required to buy a stamp to place on all official documents, including newspapers, marriage licenses, college diplomas, ships' papers, and legal records. England intended to use the money raised through the tax to help pay the costs of keeping British soldiers in America.

Many colonists rebelled. They argued that only their own elected assembly—not the British Parliament—had the right to impose a direct tax. Cries of "no taxation without representation" rang out at public gatherings. Secret rebel groups formed, calling themselves the Sons of

Liberty. Their speeches and writings inspired angry mobs, who attacked the homes of tax collectors.

The leaders of the Sons of Liberty called on colonists to boycott, or refuse to buy, British goods. Trade between England and the colonies fell sharply. At last, one year after the tax went into effect, Parliament gave in to rebel demands and repealed, or canceled, the Stamp Act.

One of the most powerful leaders in the battle against the Stamp Act was a not-too-successful businessman named Samuel Adams. As a young man, Adams had gotten a personal taste of British rule, and it was a lesson he would never forget.

In the 1740s Samuel's father, a wealthy brewer in Boston, had founded a bank, called the Land Bank, with contributions from 800 Boston merchants. Parliament disapproved of the practices of the Land Bank and voted to put an end to it. The investors lost their money and Sam's father was nearly ruined. Sam, born into a rich family, was forced to wait tables to pay for his education. The experience filled him with hatred of the British government and with a new sympathy for ordinary people.

By 1764 Sam Adams had built up a powerful organization of colonists opposed to British rule. These people, who were prepared to preserve their independence by force if necessary, called themselves "Patriots." They were opposed by the "Loyalists," who were horrified by the thought of violence or rebellion against King George. Today, historians frequently use the word "Patriots" to describe the subjects who rebelled against the king. That's because they succeeded in their fight. But in the days prior to the end of the Revolutionary War, these Patriots were, actually, "rebels."

Through speeches and writings, Adams won many converts to the rebel movement. He persuaded his friend John Hancock, who had

A portrait of Samuel Adams, engraved when the rebel leader was an elder statesman

inherited a fortune, to invest in his cause.
Adams also gained fame throughout the colonies
by his work in organizing opposition to the
Stamp Act. More than any other single man,
Sam Adams would help pave the way for the
American Revolution.

On the same day that Parliament repealed
the Stamp Act, it passed another resolution. The
Declaratory Act stated that the British Parliament had the right to pass laws affecting the
American colonies in "all cases whatsoever."
England was declaring its power to tax its colonies. Parliament soon exercised that power. In
1767, under Prime Minister Charles Townshend,
it passed the Townshend Acts.

The Townshend Acts required the colonies to
pay duties on imported paper, paint, glass, lead,
and tea. British customs officials would have the
right to inspect ships, businesses, and even
homes to make sure the duties were being paid.
Angry colonists protested that these searches

Revolutionary leader John Hancock

were an invasion of their rights.

The Townshend Acts also took away New York's right to have an elected legislature. The New York Assembly had refused to pay the costs of keeping British soldiers in New York City, and the Townshend Acts punished the colony for that refusal. New York finally gave in to Parliament's demands, and its assembly was permitted to meet again. But the colonists hated the Townshend Acts. And more and more they hated the government that had imposed them.

Again, Sam Adams and his Sons of Liberty organized the colonists in the use of a powerful weapon—the boycott. Not only would the colonies refuse to buy imported paper, paint, glass, lead, and tea—they would not buy *anything* from England.

Americans gave up tea, their favored drink, for coffee. They began to weave their own crude fabric to make clothes. Women learned to make blouses and breeches without using English straight pins. British ships sat in colonial harbors, loaded with cargo. The colonists were determined—they would use their own native goods or they would do without.

In June 1768 colonial resentment came to a head in Boston when British officials seized John Hancock's sloop, the *Liberty*. Some historians believe the ship was full of smuggled goods, others that the British were out to get Hancock, a wealthy merchant and well-known rebel. In any case, an angry street mob quickly formed. Carrying bricks, cobblestones, and clubs as weapons, the mob forced four customs officials to flee to an island in Boston Harbor for safety. The officials asked England for additional troops to restore order in the streets. King George sent them.

In October 4,000 soldiers filed off British ships in Boston Harbor. Boston was an occupied town. Tensions grew. Colonists taunted the soldiers in their brick-red coats. As the months passed, street fights broke out between the Redcoats and Boston's citizens, and mobs cried for liberty. The stage was set for bloodshed.

On the night of March 5, 1770, a crowd gathered outside Boston's Customs House, mocking the British sentry and pelting him with rocks and snowballs. The soldier called for help. Six more Redcoats came to his aid. The mob pressed closer. Fearing for their lives, the soldiers fired. Five colonials lay mortally wounded or dead.

Word quickly spread of the riot Sam Adams called the Boston Massacre. A trial cleared the Redcoats of wrongdoing. But the event caused the colonists to resent British rule even more.

On the day of the Boston Massacre, the British Cabinet was voting to repeal all of the Townshend duties except the small tax on tea. The colonists continued to boycott tea, but they began to trade in all other goods again. For the next two years, England and her American colonies enjoyed relative peace. A shipment of tea in

1773 would change all that.

The British East India Company, which traded tea and other products from Asia, had lost most of its business because of the colonial boycott. To save the company from bankruptcy, Parliament passed the Tea Act. This allowed the East India Company to ship its tea directly from China to the colonies, without paying import duties in England. The company's tea would be cheaper than the smuggled Dutch tea the colonists had been drinking. And the king could still collect his threepence per pound tax in the colonies.

American merchants joined the Sons of Liberty in denouncing the Tea Act. The resolution gave the British East India Company a monopoly, or exclusive control, of the tea trade. Only loyal merchants approved by England would be allowed to buy the inexpensive tea. Sam Adams argued that the Tea Act would be just the first of many situations in which

England would force rebel colonists out of business.

Ships owned by the East India Company began to arrive in Boston. The Sons of Liberty refused to allow them to unload their cargo. By the end of November 1773, the *Dartmouth* was tied up to Boston's docks. A few days later, the *Beaver* and the *Eleanor* arrived. By law, the ships had only 20 days to unload. December 17 was the last day cargo could be taken off the *Dartmouth.*

On the afternoon of December 16, thousands of people flooded Boston's Old South Meeting House to listen to fiery speeches. A messenger was sent to Massachusetts Governor Thomas Hutchinson, asking him to return the tea to England. His reply came back—a firm no. Suddenly Sam Adams announced, "This meeting can do nothing more to save the country."

Adams's statement set off a series of war whoops from 150 men dressed up as Indians.

The Old South Meeting House in Boston, where some 2,000 colonials gathered to protest the Tea Act

The disguised men headed for the waterfront, and the crowd followed. That night more than 300 chests full of British tea were dumped into Boston Harbor in an act of rebellion that would be known as the Boston Tea Party.

The rebels' fate was sealed. On June 1, 1774, England declared the Port of Boston closed. No ships would be permitted to load or unload cargo in Boston Harbor until the citizens paid for the tea they had destroyed. On the day the port closed, church bells all across Boston tolled in mourning.

The Committees of Correspondence—rebel groups that reported the actions of all the Sons of Liberty—quickly spread the news. The other colonies came to the aid of Massachusetts, sending food, clothing, and money overland. With a new sense of unity, the 13 colonies began to respond as one in their battles with Parliament. When Massachusetts suffered, all the colonies suffered. When Boston Harbor was closed, all

A replica of the Beaver, *one of the ships attacked by "Indians" during the Boston Tea Party*

the colonies wanted justice. When the first man would fall on Lexington Green, it would seem as if a favored son had fallen from every town and province. England was about to engage an enemy united in its dreams of independence.

CHAPTER 3

IN JUST 24 HOURS

When King George signed the bill closing Boston Harbor in June 1774, he also replaced Governor Hutchinson. The new governor of Massachusetts, General Thomas Gage, had been Britain's military commander for all North America. Gage was married to an American woman. He fully understood the colonists' growing anti-British sentiments. For months Gage would walk a fine line, trying not to anger the people of Massachusetts while at the same time enforcing the very acts of Parliament that enraged them.

Meanwhile, through the end of 1774 and in early 1775, colonial leaders continued their work of organizing opposition to the British. In

September 1774 representatives from all the colonies met in Philadelphia for the First Continental Congress. A month later, when Gage canceled a meeting of the Massachusetts Assembly, the members met anyway and declared themselves delegates to a new and independent Provincial Congress.

At these illegal congresses, rebel leaders condemned British rule and planned a unified resistance. Throughout the colonies, local militias began to drill three times a week or more. Special units of Minutemen were organized, made up of the best of the militia, who agreed to respond to danger "on a minute's notice." Military supplies, including cannons, gunpowder, cartridges, and food, were gathered in two towns near Boston—Worcester and Concord.

Organized rebellion was growing. And General Gage was becoming more and more alarmed. Though he had the authority to arrest Sam Adams and John Hancock, the most

dangerous rebel leaders, Gage believed that
such a move would lead to armed revolt by the
colonists. Instead, he decided to concentrate on
eliminating the rebels' war supplies at Concord.

That decision laid the groundwork for a
chain of events that in just 24 hours would lead
to the first battle of the Revolutionary War.

COUNTDOWN TO WAR

Tuesday evening, April 18, 1775
Rebel committees meet in Menotomy, a town
between Boston and Lexington. That evening a
committee member heading home spots a secret
British patrol riding from Boston toward
Menotomy. He races back into town to warn the
others. After sending a messenger to warn
Adams and Hancock in Lexington, the committee members hide inside the Black Horse Tavern. They watch as the disguised British soldiers
pass through Menotomy.

April 18, 7:00 P.M.

In response to news of the British patrol, Minutemen are placed on guard outside the Reverend Jonas Clark's home in Lexington, where Hancock and Adams are staying. But the patrol passes through Lexington without approaching the Clark home.

The British soldiers are actually on their way to a spot between Lexington and Concord. There they will set up a roadblock. Their orders are to make certain no rebel messenger gets through that night to warn Concord that British troops are on the march.

10:00 P.M.

On the beach at the foot of Boston Common, 700 Redcoats assemble and begin to file into longboats for the trip across the Charles River. Lieutenant Colonel Francis Smith and Major John Pitcairn are in charge.

General Gage's choice of Smith as commander

The Hancock-Clark house in Lexington, home of revolutionary preacher Jonas Clark. On the night of April 18, 1775, Sam Adams and John Hancock were staying here.

for the Concord mission is one he will later regret. Smith is a senior officer, but he is grossly overweight and a slow thinker. Because of his

slow, deliberate manner, the crossing of the
Charles River takes two hours. Meanwhile, rebel
spies are spreading word of the mission.

11:00 P.M.

Paul Revere lands on the Charlestown side of
the Charles River. Rebels have spotted his two
signal lanterns, and they are waiting with a
horse.

Revere gallops toward Lexington to raise the
alarm. Coming to a fork in the road, he heads
toward Cambridge, but as he nears the town
line, he is nearly captured by British officers. He
wheels his horse around and rides for Medford, a
less direct route to Lexington. Revere races
through Medford and beyond, waking house-
holds along the way.

Midnight

Revere arrives at the Clark house in Lexington.
Half an hour later he is joined by William

Lexington's meetinghouse bell sounded the alarm that brought 130 Minutemen to the green.

Dawes, a second messenger sent out from Boston to Lexington, but by another route. The two couriers tell the news to Adams and Hancock, and the bell in Lexington's meetinghouse rings out. Within an hour 130 Minutemen assemble on Lexington Green under Captain John Parker.

April 19, 1:00 A.M.

Revere and Dawes start for Concord and are joined by Dr. Samuel Prescott, a Concord physician. Before reaching the town, the three riders encounter the British patrol spotted earlier outside Menotomy.

Revere is captured. Dawes escapes back to Lexington. Prescott jumps a stone wall and rides for Concord, where he raises the alarm and meetinghouse bells bring out the Minutemen. Most of Concord's military supplies already have been moved or hidden; now men hide the remaining supplies.

2:00 A.M.

All is quiet. Scouts sent out from Lexington to survey the roads return—there is no sign of the Redcoats. Captain Parker dismisses the men on Lexington Green, ordering them to return when they hear the drum call. Some go home, while others go to Buckman Tavern to await the British.

As Parker dismisses his company, the British troops are just beginning their march. After crossing the Charles River, the 700 men waded through cold marsh water to reach the road at Lechmere Point, then waited an hour while rations were distributed. Wet, tired, and irritated, they at last start for Concord.

3:00 A.M.

The British forces reach Menotomy. Bells tolling throughout the countryside have alerted Lieutenant Colonel Smith that his march is no longer secret. He sends a message to General Gage in Boston, asking for reinforcements. Then he orders Major Pitcairn and six companies ahead on a quickened march.

Meanwhile, Paul Revere's captors have

Buckman Tavern on Lexington Green, where Minutemen awaited the British troops

released him outside Lexington. Revere makes his way on foot to the Clark home to assist Adams and Hancock in their escape.

4:30 A.M.

The drum roll sounds on Lexington Green. Racing to the call, 77 simply clad farmers, merchants, and craftsmen form a straggling line under the command of Captain Parker. The clump of boots and the rattle of swords are heard as hundreds of well-trained, uniformed British soldiers run up in formation.

Major Pitcairn, approaching the green with his advance troops, spots the armed colonial militia. "Lay down your arms, you damned rebels, and disperse!" he shouts. Parker sees the hopelessness of the situation and orders his men to disperse. The Minutemen slowly begin to break ranks. Suddenly a shot rings out—no one will ever know who fired it. Both sides respond with gunfire. Within minutes eight colonists are dead and nine more are wounded. Pitcairn struggles to reassemble his excited soldiers. Finally he orders the fife and drum to play, and the Redcoats march out toward Concord. On the way, Smith's troops catch up with Pitcairn's.

7:00 A.M.

A small company of Minutemen starts out from Concord down the road to Lexington to meet the British. A mile and a half out of town, they spot them. The colonials turn back, and the Redcoats, in time to fife and drum, march toward Concord.

In Concord, the Minutemen are joined by other members of the militia, and they head out of town. They cross North Bridge, which spans the Concord River, then climb to the top of a hill overlooking the bridge. Meanwhile, the Redcoats assemble in Concord. As the townspeople flee their homes, soldiers begin to search for hidden weapons and supplies. Six companies are sent to

An early print of the Battle of Lexington

guard North Bridge, and four are sent across the bridge to search the farm of Colonel James Barrett, the commander of Concord's militia.

8:00 A.M.

British troops arrive at North Bridge. Some are stationed on the bridge and others are sent part-way up the hill on which colonial forces are assembled. Minutemen and militia arriving from surrounding towns have swelled colonial ranks to nearly 400.

9:00 A.M.

Back in Boston, a 1,000-man relief force sets out for Concord in response to Smith's call for re-inforcements. Lord Percy commands the relief column. His departure has been delayed five hours because his marching orders were mistak-enly delivered to the home of Major Pitcairn. The delay will prove disastrous for England's forces.

9:30 A.M.

From their positions on the hill outside town, the colonists spot smoke rising from a bonfire the British have made of some war supplies. Fearing that Concord homes are burning, militia commanders agree to "march into the middle of town for its defense or die in the attempt."

9:45 A.M.

Colonel Barrett gives the order to march but not to fire first. As the colonials descend the hill, the Redcoats retreat to the far side of North Bridge. The Americans close in. A British volley erupts, followed by heavy firing on both sides. Two Minutemen, Isaac Davis and Abner Hosmer, and three British soldiers fall dead.

10:00 A.M.

The colonials swarm across the bridge and the Redcoats retreat. A British messenger races back to Concord for help, but slow, heavy Colonel

Smith leads the responding troops, and they arrive too late to save North Bridge. Smith's men charge at the advancing colonials, and the Americans scatter into the hills.

11:00 A.M.
The four British companies sent to search the Barrett farm return. The troops cross the scene of death at North Bridge. They pass under the eyes of the colonials, who hold their fire.

Noon
The British begin to retreat back to Boston. Meanwhile, news of the fighting is spreading through the countryside, and militiamen continue to pour in from neighboring towns. The fast-growing colonial force follows the Redcoats to Meriam's Corner, a mile from Concord. The British cross a narrow bridge, then turn to fire a volley at the rebels. The colonials return fire, and two more Redcoats fall.

This monument at Meriam's Corner marks the point at which colonial forces from neighboring towns joined with the Concord militia and drove the British back.

1:00 P.M.

The British continue to retreat. As the troops march along the narrow country road, rebel muskets peer down at them from behind natural defenses. The Americans have no organized plan of attack. Militiamen simply wait on hilltops or behind trees or stone walls, fire at the passing troops, then run through the woods to find another good hiding place. The British, trained to stand and fight on open ground, are bewildered and horrified by this style of attack. Their progress is slowed as they keep stopping to reload their rifles, then fire at an enemy who has already slipped out of sight.

2:00 P.M.

Exhausted and desperate, their wagons overflowing with wounded and their ammunition nearly gone, the British troops near Lexington. Some begin to run. Under the guns of their own officers, the soldiers re-form ranks. At last, outside Lexington, they hear a trumpet sound: Lord Percy's reinforcements have arrived.

3:00 P.M.

Smith's exhausted troops collapse behind Lord Percy's lines. The reinforcements fire cannons at the rebels, who take cover in the hills.

3:30 P.M.

Under the protection of Percy's troops, Smith's weary men move out on the 11-mile (18-kilometer) retreat to Boston. Thousands of rebels

Old Battle Road. Under fire from both sides of the woods and behind them, British troops made their retreat.

continue their constant, deadly firing from the shelter of the woods. The Redcoats struggle along the narrow road, breaking into homes and taverns along the route to search for riflemen.

4:30 P.M.

At Menotomy, both sides suffer heavy casualties, with at least 40 Americans and 40 British dead. Much of the fighting takes place in houses.

Eighty-year-old Samuel Whittemore, who has stayed behind to defend his home, is shot, clubbed, bayoneted, and left for dead. He recovers and lives to the age of 98, declaring to the end that he'd "run the same chance again." Nine-year-old Joel Adams threatens British soldiers, who are looting the family's silver, with a licking from his father. When the British set his house on fire, Joel puts out the flames with a pot of beer.

5:00 P.M.

Lord Percy leads his men out of Menotomy. He decides to head for Boston by way of Charlestown. The colonials try to block his path, but the British, firing their cannons, force the rebels to scatter.

6:00 P.M.

The retreat continues, with colonial forces steadily growing. At Prospect Hill, the weary British catch sight of Boston, across the Charles

River. Many of the soldiers have marched nearly 40 miles (64 kilometers), with little food and no rest, since last crossing the Charles.

7:00 P.M.

In the final moments of daylight, scattered musket fire continues as Percy's troops cross the narrow strip of land into the peninsula of Charlestown. The colonials cease firing and turn back. The exhausted British troops await the arrival of boats to take them back to Boston. They have lost 73 men, 174 are wounded, and 26 are missing. Colonial losses are 49 killed, 39 wounded, and 5 missing.

As darkness sets in, few have the strength to consider the meaning of what has happened in the past 24 hours. But the battles of Lexington and Concord have set the stage for a new era in history. The British Empire is about to lose its valuable North American colonies. And a new nation will soon be born.

Historic Munroe Tavern, one of the many inns and taverns that served the bustling town of Concord

CHAPTER 4

WHY CONCORD AND LEXINGTON?

By the time the American Revolution began, Concord was nearly 150 years old. Originally named Musketaquid, the village had long been a settlement of the Nashobah Indians. In 1635 colonial settlers bought from the Indians a parcel of land "six miles square." That parcel became the first Massachusetts town to be settled inland, away from ocean flooding. Concord's first colonial residents were 12 families, an Indian trader named Simon Willard, and a preacher named Peter Bulkeley.

From its beginnings, Concord had a militia, which it depended on for protection against the Indians. Strangely enough, before the opening day of the American Revolution, that militia had already marched against the British. On April 19, 1689, a company of able-bodied men marched from Concord to Boston to join other colonists in overthrowing Sir Edmund Andros, the harsh governor of New England. No blood was shed, but Andros left the colonies and was replaced by Governor William Phips. Phips arrived from England with the charter that would establish Massachusetts as a separate province, or state.

Through the 1600s and 1700s, Concord attracted settlers because of its many vital natural resources. Located on land where three rivers joined, the town enjoyed rich fishing. There was plenty of lumber for building houses, ships, and bridges. There was an abundance of iron ore, an important mineral in early America because of its use in everything from cooking kettles to muskets. The second-oldest ironworks in Massachusetts began in Concord, helping to make the town a center for business and trade.

Concord's location, within a day's ride of

Boston, added to its importance. So did the town's designation in 1692 as a "shire town"—a place where the county court was held. Colonists having business with the court often traveled great distances and stayed in one of Concord's inns or boardinghouses.

The First and Second Provincial Congresses chose Concord as their meeting place. And in November 1774, as preparations for armed resistance against the British began, Concord was selected as one of two storage sites for ammunition and other war supplies. When General Gage decided to seize the colonists' supplies, he had to pick one of the two places— Concord or Worcester—as his target. Worcester was 48 miles (77 kilometers) from Boston, a hard, two-day march over difficult roads. Concord was only 17 miles (27 kilometers) away. To Gage, it looked like an easy target. Thus, Concord became an important place in American history.

An accident of geography placed Lexington in harm's way on the morning of April 19, 1775, for it lay in the direct path of the British march from Boston to Concord.

Lexington was a more rustic town than Concord, with less trade and only half as many citizens. It had not even been established as a separate town until 1712. Before then, Lexington was simply considered a part of nearby Cambridge. Its colonial settlers supported themselves by farming, weaving cloth, and supplying Cambridge with wood and hay.

But two things made the town important that day: an experienced militia and a rebel minister. The Reverend Jonas Clark had, for many years, preached to his followers about the evils of taxation without representation. Many of those influenced by Clark had served alongside the British, some 15 years earlier, during the French and Indian War. The survivors of that war were now the main force of Lexington's

A statue of Minuteman Captain Parker on Lexington Green honors the leader and his small group of brave men.

militia—the men who gathered under Captain John Parker on Lexington Green.

What could Captain Parker have been thinking as he stood on the green in those chilly hours before dawn? A veteran soldier and commander, Parker knew the risk he took for both himself and his men by remaining in the open with loaded weapons against a force of Redcoats. Yet, having ordered his small band of men not to fire unless fired upon, he stood his ground, for the cause of freedom.

Americans today like to think that the shots fired that day on Lexington Green and North Bridge were heard around the world. The call to democracy and freedom was about to be heard in France and elsewhere around the world—wherever tyranny threatened.

CHAPTER 5

CONCORD AND LEXINGTON TODAY

The towns of Concord and Lexington have changed a lot since the Revolutionary War. Gone, for the most part, are the wide open hills and meadows. More than 45,000 people now live in the two towns, and buildings line the paved roads and highways. Concord and Lexington are "commuter towns," or suburbs of Boston. For workers traveling by car to and from their Boston jobs, the journey that took the British army an entire night now takes only 30 minutes.

But even today, much still connects these two towns to the early dreams of American liberty. A replica, or close copy, of Concord's North Bridge still stands. The National Park Service operates a visitor center in the fields

The Visitor Center at North Bridge

At the far end of North Bridge, near the place where Abner Hosmer and Isaac Davis fell, a bronze Minuteman gazes down at all who pass.

where Minutemen gathered to watch the Redcoats holding the bridge. At the far end of North Bridge, near the spot where Abner Hosmer and Isaac Davis fell, a heroic bronze

A tablet at North Bridge honors the British dead.

Minuteman surveys all who cross. Nearby a tablet marks the graves of the British soldiers who died that historic day.

Another Minuteman stands guard at the foot of Lexington Green. A few steps behind the statue, visitors can see Buckman Tavern, where the militia passed the early-morning hours waiting for the drum roll to call them to battle. Several other colonial Lexington taverns remain open to the public, as does the Hancock-Clark House, where Sam Adams and John Hancock watched their plans for revolution come to life.

Each year on Patriots' Day—the Monday nearest April 19—thousands of Massachusetts residents relive the battles of Lexington and Concord. At North Bridge, ceremonies are held to honor the men who fell there. And on Lexington Green, the public watches as modern-day "Minutemen" and a company of "Redcoats" clash again in the early-morning sun.

What happened on April 19 more than 200

The Old Manse in Concord, home of rebel Minister Waldo Emerson

years ago remains very much a part of people's lives today. In Concord and Lexington, museums, monuments, parades, and the colorful Fife and Drum Corps all do their part to preserve the

Each year on Patriots' Day, Massachusetts residents relive the events of April 19, 1775.

legacy of our colonial forefathers. But more than that, it is the hearts of Americans in New England and across the nation that help keep the spirit of liberty alive.

Concord and Lexington: A Historical Time Line

1760 George III becomes king of England.

1763 The French and Indian War ends with a British victory, leaving England deeply in debt.

1764 England begins trying to rebuild its treasury through direct taxes on its American colonies.

1768 In response to colonial protests, England sends 4,000 Redcoats to keep order in Boston.

1770 The Boston Massacre increases colonial resentment of British rule.

1773 Rebel colonists stage the Boston Tea Party to protest the Tea Act.

1774 The Continental Congress and Massachusetts Provincial Congress meet and plan a unified resistance.

1775 On April 19, colonial militiamen and Minutemen clash with British forces in Lexington and Concord, launching the Revolutionary War.

1783 The American Revolution ends. The United States is a new and independent nation.

1875 Ceremonies mark the 100th anniversary of the battles of Lexington and Concord. *The Minuteman,* a bronze statue sculpted by Concord resident Daniel Chester French, is dedicated at North Bridge.

1992 In the annual Patriots' Day celebration, Massachusetts townspeople wearing 18th-century clothing re-create the Battle of Lexington; parades and ceremonies mark the day in Concord.

Visitor Information

Concord

North Bridge Visitor Center—174 Liberty Street. Telephone number: 508-369-6993. Open every day 8:30 A.M. to 5:00 P.M. Overlooks bridge, presentations, walks, exhibits.

North Bridge—Monument Street, 3/4 mile (1.2 kilometers) north of Visitor Center. Open year-round. Site of Minuteman Statue and replica of the original bridge.

Concord Free Public Library—Main Street and Sudbury Road. Call 508-369-6240 for hours. Open year-round. Town archives, period artifacts, books, records.

Concord Museum—200 Lexington Road, ½ mile (.8 kilometer) east of Visitor Center. Telephone number: 508-369-9763. Open every day except Mondays and holidays, 10:00 A.M. to 5:00 P.M. Call to confirm times. Period rooms, galleries, artifacts from Concord homes, Paul Revere's Lantern, special exhibits.

The Old Manse—Monument Street (beside North Bridge). Telephone number: 508-369-3909. Open most days, mid-April through October, 10:00 A.M. to 5:00 P.M. Home of Revolutionary Minister Waldo Emerson.

Lexington

Battle Road Visitor Center—Route 2A, 3/4 mile (1.2 kilometers) west of Route 95. Call for times: 617-862-7753. Open mid-April through November.

Bay Road Historic Sites—Virginia Road at Route 2A. Open year-round. William Smith house and restored Hartwell Tavern.

Museum of Our National Heritage—On Route 2A at 33 Marrett Road. Call ahead: 617-861-6559. Open mid-April through October, 10:00 A.M. to 5:00 P.M. Slide show, exhibits, period artifacts.

Hancock-Clark House—36 Hancock Street (¼ mile [.4 kilometer] from green). Call ahead: 617-862-0928. Open mid-April through October, 10:00 A.M. to 5:00 P.M. Home of Reverend Jonas Clark, period rooms, details of the battle.

Buckman Tavern—Opposite Lexington's Minuteman Statue. Open mid-April through October, 10:00 A.M. to 5:00 P.M. Restored tavern where colonials awaited battle on morning of April 19, 1775.

Lexington Green—Statue of Minuteman Captain Parker. Open year-round. Seasonal reenactment.

Index